Retreat and quiet-day resource

Setting the scene for reflecting with God

SUSAN HARDWICK

Kevin Mayhew

First published in 2001 by
KEVIN MAYHEW LTD
Buxhall
Stowmarket
Suffolk IP14 3BW

© 2001 Susan Hardwick

ISBN 1 84003 720 2
Catalogue No. 1500422

9 8 7 6 5 4 3 2 1 0

Cover design by Jonathan Stroulger
Edited and typeset by Margaret Lambeth

Printed in Great Britain

CONTENTS

INTRODUCTION

A glance in journals such as *Retreats*, the annually published comprehensive list of places offering retreats of all kinds and lengths, will indicate how wide a choice exists. There seems to be something to suit every need.

Offering residential or day retreats, many of these places are happy to put together a programme that suits a group's particular requirements. However, many groups prefer to do their own designing, arranging and running of the programme.

This book will be useful for the above categories, as well as for those who wish to organise the whole event themselves at their own venue.

A retreat is a time to step aside from our everyday activities and preoccupations – maybe only for a few hours, maybe for a few days – in order to just 'be' with God.

It is a time to stop, to re-create, and to be re-created. In doing so, we respond to God's call to us constantly to be changing, growing, becoming.

NOTE   In order to simplify the text, the word, 'retreat', will be used to cover every type of event and will be qualified where necessary to indicate a particular length or style of retreat.

WHAT IS A RETREAT?

A retreat is a time to step aside from our everyday activities and preoccupations in order to just 'be' with God. It is a time to stop and to re-create.

In Genesis, the story of Creation tells how God created order out of chaos. A retreat is an opportunity to look at our own inner chaos – our attitudes, negative feelings, areas of hurt and anger – to offer it all up to God and to ask him to help us create order; to re-create ourselves just a little bit. In doing this we respond to God's call to us to constantly change and grow with him.

All through the Bible we read of people going away, or retreating, to be alone with God. Moses went to the top of Mount Sinai to receive God's covenant with his people. The prophet Elijah sat on his mountain, fasting and waiting on God and found him, not in the strong wind, earthquake or fire, but in 'a still small voice'. And as we are exhorted in Psalm 46:10: 'Be still, and know that I am God.'

The Gospels tell us that Jesus' whole life and ministry was soaked with prayer, and that he often went away to be quiet on his own. He also urged his disciples to 'come apart to a lonely place' to renew themselves in silence and in prayer. And, through-out the centuries, Christians have found it important to follow the example Jesus set.

It may not be a total coincidence that, in the headlong rush and bustle of modern-day living, retreats are becoming ever more popular as people step aside from it all for a precious while in order to experience peace and stillness and to deepen their knowledge of God.

The experience will be different for each person, because each person is unique and so has a unique relationship with God.

However, there are three basic components to every retreat experience: God, self and other people.

Often, with the luxury of time that there is on retreat, we can experience God, and his love and acceptance of us, in far greater depth than is normally possible in the busyness of our everyday lives. God is found both 'out there,' and 'in here' in our inner self. He is the wellspring within, from which we draw all our creativity and potential.

Greater awareness of God and of ourselves leads automatically to greater awareness of others, and of sensitivity to their needs.

DIFFERENT KINDS OF RETREAT

As has been said already, there are many different ways of making a retreat: there are no hard and fast rules about venue, style, length or content.

Below are listed some of the more common ones:

CONDUCTED OR PREACHED RETREATS

Although one of the most traditional, it is still the most widely used. The retreat is planned round a series of addresses designed to provide the participants, or retreatants, with material for their individual and communal meditations and prayers. There is also corporate worship. The most usual length is two to four days. Silence is usually observed throughout the main part of the retreat.

PRIVATE RETREAT

Made by an individual, usually at a retreat house or with a religious order where there is the opportunity both to share in the corporate worship, and to receive spiritual guidance when required.

More and more frequently, though, people are choosing to go on private retreats at some simple accommodation or hermitage set aside for this specific purpose, often in the grounds of a retreat house or religious order.

DROP-IN RETREATS

These may extend over a period of days, each day having a set pattern of meditations, talks, silence and, maybe, other activities. It is particularly designed for those whose commitments prevent them from being absent from home or work for an extended period. People 'drop in' each day for one or more sessions, each of which is an entirety in itself, the whole building up into a total retreat experience.

HOME RETREATS

These usually extend over a period of some weeks and they are for people who wish to make a retreat at home.

The participants meet once a week in one or another's home in order to share individual and corporate experiences and to pray. The retreat leader will give the retreatants meditation material to use in the coming week.

This type of retreat helps strengthen and develop the prayer life of each individual. Support and fellowship is provided within the group through the shared experience.

QUIET DAYS/DAY RETREATS

These can follow a wide variety of programmes and input. They are designed for those who are new to retreats and who are nervous about committing themselves initially to a more lengthy retreat, as well as for those who are unable to make a more lengthy retreat because of personal or work commitments.

There are usually addresses, times for prayer, periods of silence, and often experiential material. They may also contain activities such as drawing, painting or working with clay, the making of collages and other imaginative works of creativity.

TOWN OR CITY RETREAT

This is an example of an experiential retreat. Instead of withdrawing to a quiet place, the retreatants go out to seek meditative experience of God in the midst of the noise and crowds and bustle of the busy town or city.

INDIVIDUALLY DIRECTED RETREATS

These are based on the Spiritual Exercises of St Ignatius of Loyola, and have become enormously popular over the past 25 years. The exercises were originally designed to be given over 30 days, but now are usually given over a period of six to eight days.

The exercises provide the ground plan and, as the title suggests, the retreat giver works with the individual retreatant, each day providing him or her with material from the Gospels for contemplative meditation. The retreat giver and retreatant meet at a set time each day to discuss the fruit of these meditations.

It is usually a very in-depth, and often life-changing, experience, the retreatant being led to review his or her life in the light of the Gospel and to seek God's guidance for the future.

It is a particularly good type of retreat to undertake at times of great decision-making; the retreatant reaches deep within and is encouraged to discern how personal perceptions and motivations can affect responses to life and God's call.

As may be seen from the above, the main criterion of any retreat is to create an opportunity and environment where people can step aside for a period of time just to 'be' with God.

Everything else should be geared to enabling this.

'BE STILL, AND KNOW'

A few suggestions for those finding it difficult to relax and to concentrate.

STILLNESS AND SILENCE

In our busy and fast-moving world, stillness and silence is something most of us practise too little. Perhaps we fear the absence of noise, of distraction, and of being alone just with ourselves.

But stillness is, in fact, the opposite of absence.

Stillness is filled with presence. True stillness can be found, not just in peace and quiet, but in the midst of hustle and bustle and noise. I imagine most of us could name people we know who seem to have this inner stillness in whatever situation they find themselves; who, at the same time, still manage to engage fully with the people and events around them. One only has to watch children lost in their daydreams, totally absorbed, totally still, to see that it is an ability with which we are born.

Sadly though, somewhere on the way to adulthood, we usually lose this precious gift. So we have to rediscover and relearn it and find again that inner place of stillness to which we can return whenever we need to be nourished. It is in this place that we connect most intimately with the God-in-us; so the place of stillness also becomes the wellspring of life.

The paradox about stillness and silence is that there is so much that can be said about it!

STILLING DOWN

It is hard to concentrate our minds and to pray when our bodies are restless. If this is the case for you, try the following:

Sit in a comfortable, supportive chair, with your legs uncrossed and hands resting in your lap.

Close your eyes and concentrate first on making your breathing steady and even. In your mind work your way down your body, beginning at the top of your head and concentrating on each area.

Imagine any area in which you notice tension as a block of ice, a knotted rope, or a coiled spring. Then imagine it melting, unravelling, and loosening. Return to your breathing. As you breathe in, think the word 'Jesus'. As you breathe out, think the word 'me'.

This, in itself, is a prayer.

Now you are relaxed, just listen to what God wants to say to you in the silence of your heart. If you want to speak to him, do so.

USING THE TIME OF SILENCE CREATIVELY

- Put aside the idea that the time has to be 'useful'. Instead, hand it over to God. Sit, kneel or lie down and wait for God to lead, to speak, to put ideas, thoughts and prayers into your mind.

- Relax into the luxury of having all the time in the world just to be with God.

- If you find doing absolutely nothing impossible, try reading a passage from the Bible, some poetry, prayers or hymns. If a particular word or phrase stands out for you, stop and reflect on it. Allow the words to sink into your mind and your heart, and use it as a stepping stone into prayer.

- Similarly, pictures, photos and paintings can be a great trigger for prayer, particularly if you are a very visual person.

- Make use of the sense of touch. Hold and feel stones, or pieces of wood, and be aware of their unique shapes and textures. If the equipment is available, make something with some clay, or paint or draw.

- Walk around outside, opening up your senses to absorb the smells, sounds and sights surrounding you. Be aware of God's creative power running through everything.

- A retreat is the perfect time to face up to yourself and your particular needs. Trust that God will deal with these if you ask him to, and if you give him the time and the space. Don't forget that you need to ask, but you also need to listen for and to the answers – and to be prepared to act upon them.

- Delight in the day and all that it brings. Do not be worried if you experience ups and downs of emotions and feelings: they just show that you are allowing yourself to be vulnerable and open, which is good. Offer it all up to God. Ask him to walk through these emotions and feelings together with you, so that the light of his wisdom may shine into the dark places and give you understanding and peace.

SOME WAYS TO PRAY

The first thing to realise is that there is no set way to pray, nor a set type of prayer.

There is just one rule: we must always try to be totally honest in our prayer; to speak it just the way it really is, whether it is a shout of pain, anger or bewilderment, a cry of joy and thanksgiving, or a request for ourselves or for someone else.

As individual and unique people, we each have an individual and unique relationship with God; as unique and unrepeatable as our own set of fingerprints or DNA.

Prayer, in fact, begins with God and not with ourselves. We are reminded of this by what Jesus said in John 15:16:

'You did not choose me, but I chose you . . . '

God is constantly praying in us, speaking to us, and softly knocking on the door of our hearts. When we feel the urge to pray, we are answering this invitation.

It is all too easy to do all the talking. However, it is so important that we don't. We need to give God a chance to speak to us. Like a conversation between friends or loved ones, there should be a fair share of speaking and of listening. And, once we can get in the habit of listening to God, most probably we will often be very surprised at what he has to say to us.

Prayer is both the easiest and the hardest thing in the world – hard because it demands honesty and commitment, and easy because it is like coming home to an infinitely loving parent. With this parent, we can be confident that we can say whatever we feel at the deepest part of our being, knowing that whatever we do say will be understood, valued and treasured.

Like anything worthwhile, prayer does need working at if we are going to get deeper and deeper in to our relationship with God. However, the results can be amazing and totally life-changing.

One way to begin is just to open our mind and heart, and to say exactly how we feel with total rawness and honesty; to lay it all out before God and ask for his understanding and wisdom, his strength and healing to come into all things and situations; and for those same qualities of God to be his gift to us.

Another creative way to pray is to take a few words of Scripture which are meaningful for you, and to do the relaxation as described above. Then let the words dwell in your mind and sink into your heart, allowing their deeper meaning to speak uniquely to you and your situation.

One of our greatest God-given gifts is our imagination. Use it. Allow it to roam as wide and wild as it likes. Picture any situation, of your own or in the wider world.

Or take a passage from one of the Gospels and imagine yourself there. Picture yourself and Jesus together in the situation. What do you say to him? What is he saying to you?

God can be found in all things, for example, a photograph, a picture, a lit candle, an object that you look at or hold, or newspapers. All can be aids to getting yourself into prayer.

Get out into the fresh air, and walk. As you walk, raise your level of consciousness so that you are acutely aware of, and absorbing, your surroundings. If in the country, observe the tiny flowers, the butterflies and insects, every detail. If in a built-up area, allow it to speak to you as it will, remembering that God is everywhere and in all things.

For Jesus, prayer was a way of life. Being rooted in prayer gave him the knowledge of God's will, and the wisdom, direction, strength and courage that he needed.

Prayer can be the same for us too, if we let it.

ORGANISING A RETREAT OR QUIET DAY

There can be few events which are as likely to deepen and enrich and change people's lives profoundly in a short period of time as a retreat. So every moment of time and energy invested by the organiser(s) is time well spent.

A retreat requires that the participants commit themselves to stepping aside from their normal everyday preoccupations and activities for a period of time in order to concentrate wholly upon God.

The number one priority should be to surround the whole event, from conception to actuality, in prayer. As the psalm says:

If God doesn't build the house,
the builders only build shacks.
If God doesn't guard the city,
the night watchman might as well nap.
It's useless to rise early and go to bed late,
and work your worried fingers to the bone.

(Psalm 127:1, 2a, The Message)

Secondly, smooth unobtrusive planning and sound organisation are vital. Time spent planning at the beginning builds on the foundations laid down in the psalm above.

PRELIMINARY PREPARATIONS AND ARRANGEMENTS

DATE   Fix the date well in advance and advertise it with posters, flyers, and announcements.

COST   Will this be partly/fully subsidised for certain people, or not? Make it clear from the beginning in any publicity how much people will have to pay, and who is eligible for reduced rates.

VENUE   Decide on the venue as early as possible. The style of retreat will largely be dictated by the venue, so this needs to be clarified early on.

Points to check

- Opportunities for movement inside and, if possible, for wandering outside.
- Provision of enough comfortable seating.
- Warmth factor.
- Catering facilities appropriate to length of retreat, ensuring that it will not impinge upon the quiet. Also opportunities to make coffee/tea as required.

CONTENT

Be clear about the sort of retreat it is.

For example, will there be opportunities and encouragement for participants to draw, paint, or make collages, etc.? Or will participants be encouraged to just be quiet with God?

LENGTH

Be clear about the length of time expected participants can cope with. It is better that they come away yearning for more than relieved it is over, at long last.

WHO IT IS FOR

Who is the retreat for? Decide on your target clientele.

Target those whom you feel would especially benefit, and encourage them to sign up.

NUMBERS

Be clear about maximum numbers able to participate within the chosen venue. Don't be tempted to go above this; if it is too crowded, it will be very difficult for the participants to find interior as well as exterior space.

WHAT IT IS

Be sure that everyone understands what a quiet day or retreat involves.

Dispel any anxieties or fears. Excite people with a vision of what might happen.

See 'What is a retreat?', page 7 and 'Different kinds of retreat', page 8.

TO SPEAK OR NOT TO SPEAK

Decide whether it will be partly, or wholly, in silence. In our noisy world, even small amounts of silence can seem threatening to those who are not used to it.

Reassure any who are worried that they may not be able to cope with the silence, that many people feel this way. Explain that there is a variety of ways in which silence can be used, and that they will probably not want to come out of the silence once they have experienced it.

See 'Stillness and silence' on page 11 and 'Some suggestions for using the time of silence creatively' on page 12.

PRACTICALITIES

PUBLICITY

- Posters

- Flyers (There is a *pro-forma* flyer in the Appendix.)

- Booking forms (Don't forget a section for participants to indicate any special needs, e.g. dietary or access.)

- Signing up (Deposit or full amount required? – There is a *pro-forma* booking form in the Appendix.)

VENUE

- Check that the venue can accommodate the access needs of all participants.

- Walk round the venue and be clear which space will be used for what. With a bit of imagination, even a church hall can be turned into a very appropriate venue.

- Specific areas can easily be created for the different activities and requirements. Just a few chairs turned inwards would be sufficient to mark a boundary.

You will need

1 A worship area

- It is important to have an area which is the focal point of the retreat. It can be just a simple table with a cross, flowers, or candles; and maybe some items to aid meditation, for example icons, pictures, pebbles, or twigs.

- If celebrating Holy Communion you will need bread, wine, a chalice, a patten, service books/sheets, hymnbooks/sheets, and a Bible.

- Plan an area in front of the table/altar where people can lay their offerings of pictures drawn or painted; prose or poetry written; pebbles, flowers, twigs, etc. collected during the retreat. The worship area then reflects the journey the participants are making and what has been meaningful for them.

- Music: Book the pianist, guitarist, or other in good time. If using tapes or CDs, check there is a power point nearby, or within reach of an extension lead.

2 Seating area

If the retreat is to last more than a few hours, it is extremely important that the seating is comfortable and informal, and not cramped. Participants need to be able to find their own space in order to be alone with God.

All sorts of things can be pressed into service in order to provide informal seating. For example, large cushions scattered on mats or carpeting on which people can sit, curl up, recline or lie down; or garden recliners.

3 Refreshment area

For serving tea/coffee etc.

4 Eating area

Is this to be different from the refreshment area? Decide where people will sit when eating.

If participants are allowed to talk during the meals, allocate a table/part of a table for those who wish to remain in silence. Clearly indicate where this is.

5 Catering

Decide who is responsible for:

- Providing and/or cooking food and clearing up
- Providing cutlery, crockery and glasses
- Tea and coffee (Is this to be served at specific times, or will retreatants help themselves as required? If the former, make it clear when those times will be.)

For a part-day, or a day retreat, participants can either bring their own packed lunch, or bring a designated dish for a bring-and-share meal. If lunch and supper is required, both of the above would be an easy and economical way of catering.

6 Resource area

Equipment provided could include:

Bibles; poetry, prayer and other books as aids to meditation; paper, pens, colouring pencils, paint, collage materials, scissors and glue.

7 *Activity area*
Equipment provided could include:

Books, paper, pens, pencils, or colouring pencils; materials for collages; scissors and glue, and table/s for the above.

8 *Meditation points*
Place various artefacts at different points around the venue. For example, pictures, quotes, flowers, pebbles, icons, candles, or statuettes.

9 *Places to wander outside*
With a bit of imagination, even a very small area can be transformed into a walk of meditation (see page 21).

WALK OF MEDITATION

A SUGGESTION FOR TURNING A VERY LIMITED OUTDOOR SPACE INTO AN AREA WHERE PEOPLE CAN WANDER AND REFLECT AND PRAY.

1 Mark out the boundary in some way, e.g. with pots of flowers at each corner.

2 Mark out a path: for example, with sticks in small flowerpots linked by brightly coloured twine, which curves around, maximising the available space.

3 Along the way, place as wide a variety as possible of items which can act as points of reflection and meditation. Try to make them engage as many of the senses as possible.

The following could be used:

- quotations
- icons
- pictures
- arrangements of pebbles and/or twigs
- painted stones
- small branches of unusual shapes planted in pots; painted, or left as natural
- dried or fresh flower arrangements
- various items in bowls, e.g. flower petals, sand, pot-pourri, etc., that people can touch or smell
- bowls of water with brightly coloured marbles, pieces of coloured glass, or pebbles
- carvings
- pots of herbs and lavender
- a tape of natural sounds, with a picture of the particular sound, e.g. the sea.

If possible, create 'surprises' which are not visible from the beginning, for example, use stones or pieces of wood to create small arbours for some of the above items, so that they can be discovered as people wander around.

Indeed, almost any item, if placed in an unusual context and displayed imaginatively, can be an aid to meditation on the richness, variety and immense diversity of God's creation.

Very little is needed, if imagination and lateral thinking are employed, in the use and arrangement of what is available.

A walk of meditation can quite easily be created inside, in a single space, or by using different rooms with a particular 'mood' being expressed in each. And, of course, a church provides the perfect setting for a walk of meditation.

The following walk of meditation is a detailed example, from my own experience, of how a particular theme was treated.

WALK OF MEDITATION – AN EXAMPLE IN DETAIL

JOURNEYING IN THE FOOTSTEPS OF JESUS

THE SITUATION

This walk of meditation was part of a 'quiet day' which had to be run on a very small budget.

The organisers got a terrific 'buzz' from helping to create an extraordinary environment from a very ordinary setting, using everyday materials. All were pleasantly surprised by their own inventiveness and creativity.

The participants said they found the day, and particularly the walk of meditation, very moving and relevant because it had been in the ordinary, everyday setting in which they live, and because ordinary, everyday items had been pressed into service and given a new expression.

THE SETTING

A roughly square area, enclosed and concreted, outside a church hall.

PLANNING AND LAYOUT

The walk had been planned, as far as possible, to be authentic to the sequence of events as told in the Gospels and to represent the actual location of the places. For example, Cana was followed by Tabgha, which was followed by the Sea of Galilee and then the Mount of Beatitudes.

In order to place Nazareth in roughly the right place geographically, 'pilgrims' started near the middle of the area used, at Nazareth. They then moved to the edge of the area, to Bethlehem.

Their progression from there was in a winding, but generally clockwise direction, arriving at the Sea of Galilee diagonally opposite in the far corner, having gone via the River Jordan, the Desert, Cana and Tabgha. Their journey continued to Jerusalem via the Mount of Beatitudes, Mount Tabor, and the Mount of Olives.

The route the pilgrims were to take was marked on either side with pebbles, the occasional small pot of flowers, miniature firs or cacti. In the middle of the area, we placed some large pots of grasses, trailing plants and cacti, with arrangements of rocks and stones.

Pictorial pilgrims' maps of the Holy Land can be obtained from Christian tour companies. It will very much enhance the experience if one of these can be put up on a wall near the beginning of the walk.

STOPPING PLACES

For each stopping place, we painted the name and heading on a rough piece of wood, log or stone. The colour of the paint reflected the mood of that particular place, i.e. 'Jerusalem' was blood red; the 'Mount of Olives' was olive green; the 'Mount of Beatitudes' – grass green; the 'Sea of Galilee' – blue; 'Cana' – wine red; 'Bethlehem' – white; 'Tabgha' – wheat yellow; and 'Mount Tabor' – sunshine yellow.

Behind each sign was a display, again reflecting the prevailing mood or principal event of that place. For example, at Bethlehem there was a rough manger (made by nailing a few pieces of wood together and placing in some dried grass).

At the Mount of Beatitudes there was a mound of earth with flags stuck in, on each of which was written one of the Beatitudes.

At the Sea of Galilee we placed a container of water on which floated a simple 'biblical-style' boat. A large shell was placed beside the container so that the water could be stirred or scooped.

Another mound of earth represented Jerusalem, on the summit of which were three crosses. On the near side, a path wound up to the crosses. On the far side, at the base of the mound, a recess had been scooped out to represent the empty tomb, and just by that some small pots of bright flowers had been sunk in the earth to represent the garden where Jesus appeared to Mary Magdalene after his resurrection.

We also had both a main text and a background text.

Along our walk the main text was written or painted on whatever material seemed most appropriate for that particular place, i.e. a stone, a laminated card (a clear plastic envelope or sandwich bag could be used), or a piece of cloth.

The background text was printed onto sheets of paper and 'pilgrims' collected a copy before they started their pilgrimage. However the main text could equally well be printed if there is not enough time to prepare it in the way that we did.

Most of the preparatory work was done by various people at times suited to themselves and so the workload was spread. It did not take much time to assemble the walk of meditation, as we had a clear plan before we started about what was going where.

A DETAILED PLAN OF THE LAYOUT

NAZARETH

Main text

MARY SAYS 'YES'.

'The Holy Spirit will come upon you, and the power of the Most High will overshadow you. So the holy one to be born will be called the Son of God.'
'I am the Lord's Servant,' Mary answered. 'May it be to me as you have said.'
(Luke 1:35, 38)

(Background text: Luke 1:26-38)

Here also, Jesus grows to manhood (Luke 2:41-end). Later on, he is rejected by those amongst whom he grew up. (Luke 4:14-30)

BETHLEHEM

Main text

'TODAY, IN THE TOWN OF DAVID, A SAVIOUR HAS BEEN BORN TO YOU; HE IS CHRIST THE LORD.'

While Mary and Joseph were in Bethlehem, the time came for Jesus to be born, and she gave birth to her firstborn, a son. She wrapped him in cloths and placed him in a manger, because there was no room for them in the inn. (Luke 2:6,7)

Shepherds and kings came to worship the child, Jesus.

(Background text: Luke 2:4-21 and Matthew 3:1-13)

THE RIVER JORDAN

Main text

JESUS IS BAPTISED

As he was praying [after his baptism], heaven was opened and the Holy Spirit descended on him in bodily form like a dove. And a voice came from heaven: 'You are my Son, whom I love; with you I am well pleased.'
(Luke 3:21-23)

(Background text: John 1:29-34)

THE DESERT

Main text

FORTY DAYS AND FORTY NIGHTS

Then Jesus was led by the Spirit into the desert to be tempted by the devil.
(Matthew 4:1)

(Background text: Matthew 4:1-11)

After this, Jesus begins his public ministry of preaching, teaching, healing and raising.

CANA	**JESUS CHANGES WATER INTO WINE**
Main text	*This, the first of his miraculous signs, Jesus performed at Cana in Galilee. He thus revealed his glory, and his disciples put their faith in him.*
	(John 2:11)
	(Background text: John 2:1-11)

TABGHA	**JESUS FEEDS THE FIVE THOUSAND**
Main text	*Taking the five loaves and two fish and looking up to heaven, he gave thanks and broke the loaves. Then he gave them to his disciples to set before the people; he also divided the two fish among them all. They all ate and were satisfied.*
	(Mark 6:41, 42)
	(Background text: Mark 6:30-44)
	After his death, Jesus appears to his disciples at Tabgha (John 21:1-24).

THE SEA OF GALILEE	**JESUS CALMS ITS STORMY WATERS**
Main text	The disciples' boat was buffeted by winds. During the night, Jesus went out to them, walking on the lake. The disciples, thinking he was a ghost, cried out in fear.
	But Jesus immediately said to them, 'Take courage. It is I. Don't be afraid.'
	'Lord, if it's you,' Peter replied, 'tell me to come to you on the water.'
	'Come,' he said.
	Then Peter got down out of the boat, walked on the water and came towards Jesus. But when he saw the wind he was afraid and, beginning to sink, cried out, 'Lord, save me!'
	Immediately Jesus reached out his hand and caught him. 'You of little faith,' he said, 'why did you doubt?'
	And when they climbed into the boat, the wind died down.
	(Matthew 14:24-32)
	(Background text: Matthew 14:22-33)

THE MOUNT OF BEATITUDES	**JESUS PREACHES THE SERMON ON THE MOUNT**
Main text	*When he saw the crowds, he went up on a mountainside and sat down . . . and he began to teach them . . . When Jesus had finished . . . the crowds were amazed at his teaching, because he taught as one who had authority, and not as their teachers of the law.*
	(Matthew 5:1, 2; 7:28, 29)
	(Background text: Matthew 5:1-7:29)

MOUNT TABOR	**JESUS IS TRANSFIGURED**
Main text	*His face shone like the sun, and his clothes became as white as the light.* *(Matthew 17:2b)* (Background text: Matthew 17:1-13)

THE MOUNT OF OLIVES

Main text	*Jesus said, 'O Jerusalem, Jerusalem, you who kill the prophets and stone those sent to you, how often I have longed to gather your children together, as a hen gathers her chicks under her wings, but you were not willing!'* *(Luke 13:34)* (Background text: Luke 13:31-end)
Main text	*[After the Last Supper], they went to a place called Gethsemane, and Jesus said to his disciples, 'Sit here while I pray.'* *(Mark 14:32)* (Background text: Mark 14:32-41)
Main text	*'Rise!' Jesus said. 'Let us go! Here comes my betrayer!'* *(Mark 14:42)*

JERUSALEM	**JESUS' PASSION CONTINUES. HIS DEATH AND RESURRECTION**
Disowned	Jesus is disowned by Peter. (Luke 22:54-62)
Mocked	Jesus is mocked by the guards. (Luke 22:63-65)
Tried and condemned	Jesus is tried by Herod and Pilate, and condemned to death. (Luke 22:66-23:25)
Crucified	Jesus is led away and crucified. (Luke 23:26-56)
Resurrection	Mary Magdalene went to the disciples with the news, 'I have seen the Lord!' (John 20:18a) (Background text: John 20:1-21:25)

As the 'pilgrims' finally left the courtyard, they came face to face with a sign that said:

'I am with you and will watch over you wherever you go.'
(Genesis 28:15)

'And look, I am with you always;
yes, to the end of time.'
(Matthew 28:20b, *New Jerusalem Bible*)

PLANNING THE PROGRAMME

This requires some sensitivity in order to accommodate and reflect the various needs of those taking part. It is important to strike the balance between overloading the time and leaving acres of space which some might find threatening.

At the beginning of the retreat, put up a copy of the timetable at a central point, so it can easily be referred to.

Expect everyone to come to the Alpha and Omega inputs (see pages 31-34), and to the Holy Communion if you are having a celebration. However, unless it is essential to making sense of the retreat, make it clear that participants may choose whether or not to attend the Worship and Reflection input (see pages 31-33). They may have embarked upon a separate journey with God, and so may find the addresses distracting.

If the retreat giver is offering slots where retreatants can come to see him or her to talk about any particular issue raised by the retreat, it is a good idea to put up a list of times which people can tick rather than writing their names. This helps to preserve confidentiality. It is also a good idea to make these slots no more than 15 minutes long, in order to keep the conversation focused.

Make it clear at the beginning of the retreat that these slots are not for in-depth discussions (which belong to another time) but rather for the sharing of a particular issue that has been raised for the participant by being on the retreat. Also, deep discussion can distract the retreatant from the primary task, which is a deep encounter with God and not with the retreat giver.

However, there may be occasions when someone on retreat is struggling with a serious problem which is more than the retreat giver can handle. Again, sensitivity is called for in discerning these situations and the best way in which to respond.

One of several courses of action would be appropriate:

If there are other retreatants waiting to be seen, arrange a time later when you will be able to meet with the person in order to talk in greater depth and to direct her or him towards the most appropriate help.

If there is no one else waiting to be seen, give the person enough time to share the burden on their heart and for you to understand the nature of the problem, so that you may give appropriate advice. But do not get drawn out of your depth and into the heart of the situation, for you might raise the person's expectations as to your ability to help, only to leave them 'beached'.

The word 'counselling' has become so overused these days, that it is in danger of losing its definition. What exactly constitutes 'counselling' is widely misunderstood. But there is a world of difference between a sympathetic listening ear and common-sense advice, and the level of professional counselling skills needed for people with serious problems. A good rule of thumb is, that if you are at all in doubt as to your level of skill and ability to give appropriate help, then don't. Just point the person towards the most appropriate helping agency.

The addresses and telephone numbers of the major helping agencies are listed in the front of most telephone directories. At the back of this book is a similar list.

INPUTS

WORSHIP AND REFLECTION

LENGTH

It is a good idea to keep these within 10-15 minutes if the retreat is for a day or part-day.

SUGGESTED FORMAT

- Gentle soft meditative music for participants to come in to
- Short Bible or other reading
- Short reflection
- Prayer
- Meditative music, hymn or repetitive chant, for example: 'Be still, and know that I am God.'
- Explain beforehand that this will lead everyone into the silence.

NB

At a central point put up a list of the readings to be used in case retreatants wish to use them in their own prayers and reflection.

ALPHA AND OMEGA

On the day before the retreatants arrive, make time for those doing the organising and inputs to spend a few moments in prayer together (see page 59 for a suggested prayer).

Begin on time. Hopefully, everyone has arrived, settled in and had a cup of coffee. Now they are gathered together for the start of the retreat.

ALPHA

Begin with prayer. For a selection of opening prayers, see pages 60-63.

Practicalities

This is very important, as it sets the scene for all that is to come.

- Welcome everyone. Ask the retreatants to briefly introduce themselves and give a few details, just in case there are any in the group who don't know the others.

- Explain all the practical arrangements; check that everyone is comfortable with the plans, and knows where everything is and the times things are happening. Tell them where the timetable and any other relevant information are displayed.

- Reassure participants that they are free to wander around as they feel inclined. However, also tell them about any places where they are not able to go.

- Make it clear whether everyone is expected to come to all the inputs, or whether they are free to choose. But do emphasise that everyone should come to the final session.

- Explain what form the Worship and Reflection inputs will take, and how long each will last. Emphasise that the inputs and suggested Bible passages are there as an offering: participants should feel free to go where *God* guides, and that might be somewhere quite different.

- Pick up on any anxieties. Give the participants time to voice them. Reassure everyone that, as they have honoured God's call to them to give this time to him, God will honour them. Therefore, they should just relax into God's love and care and let him lead them to where he wants them to be.

- If you have not been able to meet prior to the retreat, it might be a good idea briefly to run through some breathing and relaxation exercises to help retreatants still themselves. It's hard to have a still mind if one's body is restless (see pages 11-12 for 'Stilling down' relaxation exercises).

- If it is a silent retreat, make it clear if meals are to be in silence as well. If they are, explain that music will be played or someone will read. If the meal is not to be in silence, explain the arrangements for those who wish to remain in silence (see page 12 – 'Some suggestions for using the time of silence creatively'). Remind everyone about the importance of keeping any silence: one person may have a need to talk but the person to whom they try to talk may want to be silent.

  The desire to talk on a silent retreat is usually driven by anxiety, or fear of the silence and how they are going to cope with it. Hence the importance of reassurance at the beginning and the facilities to help retreatants face and enter the silence in a creative way, e.g. books of meditations, poetry or reflections.

  Reassure them that once people get 'into' silence they will invariably find it surrounds them like a duvet – soft, warm, comforting and luxurious – and they will most probably be reluctant to come out from it.

- Warn participants to resist the temptation to let the retreat end early. It has so often been the case that people's profoundest experiences and insights happen in the final moments.

- Reassure participants that they should not anticipate any particular outcome. Maybe they will experience a lot, maybe very little of which they are consciously aware. But God knows best, and he moves as he will. So it is best just to trust that he will give to each according to his or her true need.

- Remind everyone that they are there in order to be alone with God and so they should set aside anything that may distract them from this central task. This includes any work or letter writing, etc., that they may have brought with them; such things should remain firmly in the briefcase or in the boot of the car. They are there to relax, reflect, pray, wander and wonder, and nothing else.

- Explain that all the worship will be led by the retreat giver, so that the participants can just give themselves totally to this time without having to concern themselves with anticipating and practising their contribution.

Worship and Reflection 1

This is a good point at which to move into the first Worship and Reflection input. If a silent retreat, remind the retreatants that this input will lead into the first silence.

OMEGA

Pulling it together

This is a time for sharing the experiences of the retreat and what it has meant for everyone. At the same time make it clear that the wishes of those who do not want to share what might be very private, and just between them and God, will be respected.

Final worship

Gather up the threads of the day in the final worship which should have a celebratory, hopeful and joyful feel to it; and should send each participant out strengthened and ready to pick up the threads of life again.

Closing prayer

For a selection of closing prayers, see pages 64-67.

The Grace

At the end of the worship, ask everyone to stand in a circle, link hands and say the words of the Grace, looking around at one another as they do so.

In this way, everyone participates in the blessing and sending out of those with whom they have been sharing what has been, hopefully, a special experience.

THEMES AND READINGS

THEME
- Choose an all-embracing theme to hold the whole retreat together and to give it a sense of unity as well as movement and progression.

- Keep it simple.

- The main purpose, the only purpose really, of a retreat of any length, is to provide the opportunity for the participants to step aside from their daily routine and to spend some time with God. Everything should be geared towards this.

- Themes which are complicated, and addresses that are too academic, distract the participants from the central focus which should be God and not the intellectual skills or erudition of the retreat giver.

READINGS
- Keep these short, especially if having more than one.

- Take care to surround the key text with only as much material as you need in order to give context.

OUTLINE THEMES AND ACCOMPANYING READINGS

The following pages contain a range of themes and appropriate readings suitable for retreats of varying lengths.

The possibilities are endless, and this is only a small selection. They are offered as just a few examples of the huge variety of sources which may be used.

1   HERE I AM, LORD!

KEY PASSAGE   ISAIAH 6:8

Then I heard the voice of the Lord saying,
'Whom shall I send? And who will go for us?'
And I said, 'Here am I. Send me!'

THEME   God reaches out to us in so many different situations and in so many different ways. Are we ready to respond as Isaiah did?

Reflection 1
Mary says 'yes'.
(Luke 1:26-38)

Are we ready to say 'yes' to God's call?

Reflection 2
The disciples leave John the Baptist in order to follow Jesus.
(John 1:19-37)

Are we prepared to leave comfortable certainties and to move on in our search for God and in order to follow him?

Reflection 3
The Potter breaks the pot and remoulds the fragments.
(Jeremiah 18:1-6a)

Are we ready to be broken and remoulded?

Reflection 4
After the feeding of the 5,000, all the fragments are gathered up; nothing is wasted.
(John 6:1-13)

Are we ready for all the disparate, fragmented parts to be gathered up, made whole, and used in God's service, so that 'nothing is wasted'?

Reflection 5
Jesus calls Lazarus – and us – out of the tomb.
(John 11:17-44)

Are we ready to be called out of the tomb of narrow thinking, prejudices and closed minds into the new life of the light and mind of Christ?

2   THE PRODIGAL SON

KEY PASSAGE   LUKE 15:11-24

THEME   From realisation to rejoicing

Reflection 1
Realisation and resolution

verses 17 and 18a (. . . to my father)

Reflection 2
Repentance and return

verses 18b (. . . and say . . .) -20a (. . . to his father)

Reflection 3
Reconciliation and reclothing

verses 20b-22

Reflection 4
Rejoicing

verses 23 and 24

Final reading
Romans 5:1-10

Peace and joy through Jesus Christ

3 THAT'S THE SPIRIT!

KEY PASSAGE   **GALATIANS 5:16-18, 22-26**

*Live by the Spirit, and you will not gratify
the desires of the sinful nature . . .
they are in conflict with each other.*

THEME   The fruits of the Spirit are love, joy, peace, patience, kindness, goodness, faithfulness, gentleness and self-control.

Conditions for bearing fruit

Reflection 1
Contact with the Living Water
(Psalm 1:3)

Reflection 2
Spiritual receptivity
(Matthew 13:23)

Reflection 3
Death of the old life
(John12:24)

Reflection 4
Being pruned
(John 15:2)

Reflection 5
Living in Christ
(John 15:5)

Reflection 6
The many varieties of fruit
(Galatians 22; 23)

Fruitfulness

Reflection 1
'I chose you . . . to bear fruit that will last.'
(John15:16)

Reflection 2
Jesus' life, death and resurrection:
so that we might bear fruit to God
(Romans 7:4)

Reflection 3
Perennial leaves and fruit of every kind
(Ezekiel 47:12)

Reflection 4
The seed grows only on good ground
(Matthew 13:8)

Reflection 5
The fruits of the Spirit are very varied
(Galatians 22-23)

Both the above may be used in a variety of ways:

- by condensing several of the reflections into one
- by picking from the above the most salient passages for your particular group and retreat
- by using the suggested passages on two interrelated retreats.

4 'I AM WITH YOU ALWAYS'

KEY PASSAGE   **MATTHEW 28:20**

*Jesus said, 'And surely I am with you always,
to the very end of the age.'*

THEME   God's faithfulness and constancy.

We are . . .

*1 . . . like branches in the vine.
(John 15:4)*

'Remain in me, and I will remain in you. No branch can bear
fruit by itself; it must remain in the vine. Neither can you bear
fruit unless you remain in me.'

*2 . . . in perpetual fellowship with Christ.
(John 17:23)*

'I in them and you in me. May they be brought to complete
unity to let the world know that you sent me and have loved
them even as you have loved me.'

*3 . . . held close by his hand.
(John 10:28)*

'I give them eternal life, and they shall never perish; no one
can snatch them out of my hand.'

*4 . . . inseparable. No power can separate us from the love
of God in Christ Jesus.
(Romans 8:38, 39)*

'For I am convinced that neither death nor life, neither angels
nor demons, neither the present nor the future, nor any
powers, neither height nor depth, nor anything else in all
creation, will be able to separate us from the love of God
that is in Christ Jesus our Lord.'

*5 . . . constantly accompanied by his Presence.
(Genesis 28:15)*

God said to Abraham,
'I am with you and will watch over you wherever you go.'

5   'WHO DO *YOU* SAY I AM?'

THEME   Jesus challenges us to declare and to confess our faith in the Son of the living God.

KEY PASSAGE   **MATTHEW 16:13-17**

When Jesus arrived in the villages of Caesarea Philippi, he asked his disciples, 'What are people saying about who the Son of Man is?'

They replied, 'Some think he is John the Baptiser, some say Elijah, some Jeremiah or one of the prophets.'

He pressed them, 'And how about you? Who do you say I am?'

Simon Peter said, 'You're the Christ, the Messiah, the Son of the living God.'

Jesus came back, 'God bless you, Simon, son of Jonah! You didn't get that answer out of books or from teachers. My Father in heaven, God himself, let you in on this secret of who I really am.'

(*The Message*)

JESUS SAID, 'I AM'

PASSAGES TO GROUP AND USE ON RETREATS OF VARYING LENGTHS

1	The Messiah	John 4:26 (4:25,26)
2	The bread of life	John 6:35 (6:32-35)
3	From above	John 8:23 (8:21-23)
4	The Eternal One	John 8:58 (8:54-58)
5	The light of the world	John 9:5 (9:1-5)
6	The gate	John 10:7 (10:1-7)
7	The Son of God	John 10:36 (10:30-36)
8	The resurrection and the life	John 11:25 (11:17-26)
9	The Lord and Master	John 13:13 (13:6-15)
10	The way, truth and life	John 14:6 (14:1-6)
11	The true vine	John 15:1 (15:1-5a)
12	The Alpha and the Omega	Revelation 1:8 (1:4-8)
13	The First and the Last	Revelation 1:17 (1:10,12-18a)

SUGGESTED GROUPINGS

a Nos. (1), 2, 5, 11, 13

b Nos. 2, 8, 10, (13)

c Nos. 4, 6, 7, 9

A SAMPLE PROGRAMME FOR A WEEKEND RETREAT

THEME: 'COME, FOLLOW ME'

FRIDAY EVENING	Arrive and settle in
6.30pm	Dinner
8pm	Alpha
8.30pm	**Worship and Reflection 1**

Music
Reading: Luke 5:1-11 – the call of the disciples
Reflection
Prayer
Hymn: *Jesus, stand among us*

This leads into the silence

(If the whole retreat is not to be in silence, go into silence from the end of the Worship and Reflection until after breakfast on Saturday.)

SATURDAY	
8.30am	Breakfast
9.30am	**Worship and Reflection 2**

Reading: I Kings 19:9-13 – Elijah and the still small voice of God
Hymn: *Open our eyes, Lord*

Private prayer and reflection

11am	Coffee

Private prayer and reflection

12.15pm	Eucharist
	Readings:
	Isaiah 6:1-8 – the call of Isaiah
	I Peter 5:1-11 – instructions to the faithful
	Luke 24:13-35 – the road to Emmaus
	Hymns: *How lovely on the mountain*
	I, the Lord of sea and sky
1pm	Lunch
	Private prayer and reflection
4pm	Tea
	Private prayer and reflection
5pm	**Worship and Reflection 3**
	Reading: Matthew 8:23-27 – the calming of the storm
	Hymn: *Eternal Father, strong to save* or
	Do not be afraid (When you walk through the waters)
	Private prayer and reflection
6pm	Dinner
	Private prayer and reflection
9pm	Compline

SUNDAY

8am	Breakfast
9am	**Worship and Reflection 4**
	Reading: Matthew 6:5-13 – Jesus teaches his disciples to pray
	Hymn: *Our Father, who art in heaven* or
	Thy way, not mine, O Lord
	Private prayer and reflection
11am	Coffee
	Private prayer and reflection

12 noon   Eucharist

Readings:

Isaiah 40:9-11 – comfort God's people and proclaim him as shepherd; *or*
Isaiah 43:1-3(10a) – our faithful God and Saviour who calls us by name
Luke 9:23-27 – the Transfiguration

Hymns: *Will you come and follow me if I but call your name*
Let there be love shared among us
Take my life, and let it be

1pm   Lunch

Private prayer and reflection

4pm   Omega

Final worship

The Grace: the group stand in a circle holding hands, saying the words together whilst looking round at each other

4.45pm   Tea

5pm   Depart

A VARIETY OF PROGRAMME OUTLINES

EXAMPLES OF PROGRAMMES FOR RETREATS OF DIFFERENT STYLES AND LENGTHS

PART DAY – MORNING

9.30AM TO 1PM (3½ HOURS)

9-9.20am	Arrival and tea/coffee, ready for prompt start at 9.30am
9.30-9.40am	Alpha
9.40-9.50am	**Worship and Reflection 1**
	This leads into silence
	Private prayer and reflection
10.50am	Coffee and biscuits
11-11.10am	**Worship and Reflection 2**
	Private prayer and reflection
12.15-12.40pm	Holy Communion
	If you are not having a service of Holy Communion, follow the same pattern as in Worship and Reflection, adding in a couple of hymns or pieces of music, and ending with a hopeful 'sending out' hymn.
12.40-12.55pm	Omega
12.55pm	Closing prayer
	The Grace: everyone stands, holding hands in a circle and joins in, looking round at one another as they do so.
1pm	Depart

Part day – afternoon

1pm-5pm (4 hours)

12.30-12.50pm	Arrival and tea/coffee, ready for prompt start at 1pm
1-1.10pm	Alpha
1.10-1.20pm	**Worship and Reflection 1**
	This leads into silence.
	Private prayer and reflection
2.30-2.40pm	**Worship and Reflection 2**
	Private prayer and reflection
3.20pm	Tea, biscuits/cake
	Private prayer and reflection
3.30-3.40pm	**Worship and Reflection 3**
	Private prayer and reflection
4.15-4.40pm	Shortened service of Holy Communion, ending with a celebratory and hopeful 'sending out' hymn
4.40-4.55pm	Omega
4.55pm	Closing prayer
	The Grace
5pm	Depart

OR

1-1.20pm	As above
2.45-2.55pm	**Worship and Reflection 2**
2.55-4.15pm	Private prayer and reflection
4.15-4.55pm	As above
5pm	Depart

PART DAY – EVENING

6.30-9.30PM (3 HOURS)

From 6pm	Arrival and tea/coffee, biscuits, etc., ready for a prompt start at 6.30pm
6.30-6.40pm	Alpha
6.40-6.50pm	**Worship and Reflection 1** This leads into the silence. Private prayer and reflection
7.50-8pm	**Worship and Reflection 2**
8-8.10pm	Tea/coffee and biscuits Private prayer and reflection
9-9.15pm	Omega
9.15-9.30pm	Service of Compline
9.30pm	Depart

QUIET DAY

9.30AM TO 4.30PM

From 9am	Arrival and tea/coffee, ready for prompt start at 9.30am
9.30-9.45am	Alpha
9.45-9.55am	**Worship and Reflection 1**
	This leads into the silence
	Private prayer and reflection
11am	Coffee/tea, biscuits
11.15-11.25am	**Worship and Reflection 2**
	Private prayer and reflection
12.30pm	Celebration of Holy Communion
1-1.30pm	Lunch
1.30pm	Into silence
	Private prayer and reflection
2.30-2.40pm	**Worship and Reflection 3**
	Private prayer and reflection
3.30-3.45pm	Tea/coffee and biscuits/cake *or*
3.40pm	Collect tea/coffee, cake, etc., to take into . . .
3.45-4.10pm	Omega
4.10pm	Closing worship
	The Grace
4.30pm	Depart

PRAY-AND-PLAY QUIET DAY

9.30AM TO 4.30PM

From 9am	Arrival and tea/coffee ready for prompt start at 9.30am
9.30-9.45am	Alpha
9.45-9.55am	**Worship and Reflection 1**
From 9.55am	Various activities, e.g. painting, drawing, sewing, collage, clay, etc., done in the presence of the Lord, as an offering to God of our gifts.
	Decide beforehand whether there can be quiet, gentle, appropriate (i.e. no gossip!) conversation, or if the activities should be done in silence.
	Make it clear that the wish of any to be in silence should be respected if you opt for the former.
11am	Coffee/tea, biscuits
11.10am	**Worship and Reflection 2**
11.25am	Various activities, as above
12.45pm	Celebration of Holy Communion
1.15pm	Lunch
1.45pm	Enter into silence. If participants wish, activities from the morning can be continued, but in silence.
3.30pm	Items which have been worked on through the day, may be laid in front of the altar as an offering.
	Tea/coffee, biscuits, cake
3.45pm	Omega
4.15pm	Final worship
4.30pm	Depart

Continued . . .

PRAY-AND-PLAY QUIET DAY

_OR_ FROM 9.30AM TO 12.30PM AS ABOVE, THEN:

12.30pm	End of activities
12.45pm	**Worship and Reflection 3**
1pm	Lunch
1.30pm	Silence
	Private prayer and reflection
3.15pm	Offerings can be placed on the floor in front of the altar, as above
	Tea/coffee and cake
3.30pm	Omega
4pm	Celebration of Holy Communion
4.30pm	Depart

WEEKEND RETREAT

FRIDAY EVENING	Arrive and settle in
	Dinner
7.30-8pm	Alpha
8-8.15pm	**Worship and Reflection 1**
	Private prayer and reflection
9.45-10pm	Night prayers
SATURDAY	
8am	Morning prayers
8.30am	Breakfast
9.30-9.45am	**Worship and Reflection 2**
	Private prayer and reflection
12.15pm	Celebration of Holy Communion

1pm	Lunch
	Private prayer and reflection
4pm	Tea
	Private prayer and reflection
5-5.15pm	**Worship and Reflection 3**
	Private prayer and reflection
6pm	Dinner
	Private prayer and reflection
9-9.20pm	Service of Compline

SUNDAY

8am	Morning prayers
8.30am	Breakfast
9.15-9.30am	**Worship and Reflection 4**
	Private prayer and reflection
12 noon	Celebration of Holy Communion
1pm	Lunch
	Private prayer and reflection
4-4.45pm	Omega
4.45-5pm	Closing prayers and the Grace
5pm	Tea
	Depart

SILENCE It is a good idea to build some silence in, even if the whole weekend is not to be in silence. For example, silence could be observed each evening from the last prayers through until after breakfast the next morning.

TOWN OR CITY RETREAT

This has been treated in greater detail due to the unusual nature of this style of retreat.

THEME

Seeking and finding God in all places: seeking the experience of God in meditative exploration, in the midst of the noise and bustle of people, rather than in peace and quiet.

KEY PASSAGES

If I go up to the heavens, you are there;
if I make my bed in the depths, you are there.
(Psalm 139:8)

Walk about Zion, go round her, count her towers,
consider well her ramparts,
view her citadels,
that you may tell of them to the next generation.
For this God is our God for ever and ever;
he will be our guide even to the end.
(Psalm 48:12-14)

EXPLANATION

- The retreatants stay in a place which is conducive to quiet reflection and prayer.

- During the day, retreatants go out from this place into the streets of the town or city. There they mingle with people going about their daily lives, and reflect, in their own hearts and minds, on the presence and experience of God in this everyday environment – not just for themselves, but for everyone.

- They are in the town/city to receive and to absorb, not to evangelise.

- This daytime activity is framed by retreatants having the opportunity to meet together in prayer and preparation before they go out amongst the crowds.

- Similarly, at the end of the day, they come together to share their thoughts, experiences and reflections, and to pray for the people and the situations they have encountered.

- The role of the retreat giver is primarily in aiding reflection and the making of biblical and theological links with what has been experienced; to facilitate worship; to support and pray for the retreatants during the day whilst they are out 'on the town'.

- It is a good idea if silence is observed from the final corporate prayer and worship of the day until after breakfast the next morning.

A WEEKEND PROGRAMME FOR A TOWN OR CITY RETREAT

FRIDAY

6pm Arrive and settle in

6.30pm Dinner

7.30pm Welcome and discussion about the weekend ahead:
- Setting the scene
- Practical issues
- The lay of the land: simple road maps given out and clarification of areas each person has been allocated
- Expectations and apprehensions
- Questions
- Spiritual preparation

9pm **Worship and Reflection 1**
Followed by silence until after Holy Communion on Sunday

Private prayer and reflection

SATURDAY

7.30am Holy Communion

8am Breakfast

9am Joint prayer and preparation, ending with 'sending out' prayer and blessing

9.30am 'Out on the town' in ones or twos

12 noon Return for lunch, or have lunch in town as part of the experiencing of the local life

1.30pm	'Out on the town' in a different area from that experienced in the morning
4pm	Return Tea and cake, etc.
4.30pm	**Worship and Reflection 2** Private prayer and reflection
6pm	Dinner
7pm	Sharing time: • Sharing experiences, thoughts, reflections and feelings • Prayer for people and situations encountered • End this time with Compline Prayer and reflection Silence until after Holy Communion on Sunday

SUNDAY

8am	Holy Communion
8.30am	Breakfast
9.30am	'Sending out' prayer and blessing 'Out on the town' – going to different areas from the day before
1pm	Return for lunch
2pm	Sharing time: as previous day Private prayer and reflection
4.30pm	Tea and cake
4.45pm	Reflecting on the weekend
5.45pm	Final worship
6pm	Depart

SOME SUGGESTED READINGS

Deuteronomy 4:39

Psalm 139, especially verses 7-12

Psalm 48:12-14

Psalm 15:3

Isaiah 66:1, 2a

Jeremiah 23:24

Acts 17:27

SOME SUGGESTED HYMNS

God of concrete, God of steel

O Lord, all the world belongs to you

Jesus Christ is waiting, waiting in the streets

Forth in the peace of Christ we go

Christ's is the world in which we move

Be still, for the presence of the Lord

One more step along the world I go

A SELECTION OF PRAYERS

A PRAYER FOR THE ORGANISERS AND THE RETREAT GIVER

BEFORE THE RETREAT BEGINS

Ensure everyone doing the organising and inputs spend a few moments together in prayer. Place the retreat, the retreatants and everyone involved into God's care, that his will be done in and through all those who will be present.

Lord,
we have gone forward in faith
and organised this retreat,
trusting and believing that this is your will.
We have done our part
to the very best of our ability.

Now we hand the time over to you.

We ask that you will bless each one
according to their need.

Bless the retreatants
and still any anxieties they may have.
May it be a wondrous
and holy time for them.

Bless those who will be organising
the practical part.

Bless the retreat giver,
that her/his words may resonate
with that which you have begun.

Thank you for the privilege of calling us
to be part of furthering your Kingdom
in this way.
Amen.

OPENING PRAYERS

ANTICIPATION AND
APPREHENSION

Lord,
anticipation and apprehension:
two opposing feelings of equal measure
that I feel as I begin this retreat.

Anticipation of all the blessings
I know in faith will be mine.
And apprehension
because of all that your loving gaze
will light up,
and challenge
and call to change.

So help me to honour this time,
to give of my very best to you.
May it all be for your greater glory.
Amen.

BLESS THIS TIME

Bless this time, Lord.
As I have honoured
your call to come here,
so honour my obedience.
I ask this in your name.
Amen.

THERE IS TIME ENOUGH

Creator God,
it's one of the mysteries and miracles
of a retreat,
however long or short,
that there is time enough
for all you would wish to work.

So help each one here today
to remain faithful to the task;
to be co-creators with you
in bringing to life
your hopes and your dreams for us.
Amen.

WINGING, SOARING, SWOOPING SPIRIT OF GOD

Holy Spirit of God,
winging, soaring, swooping,
filling to the brim
each cup held up
in faith-fillled expectation.
Work your wonder in me.
Fill me to the brim
with your blessings,
so that I may go out from here
in Jesus' name
to be a blessing to others.
In God's name I ask it.
Amen.

TEACH US HOW TO HEAR

God of all,
sometimes in the earthquake,
sometimes in the storm;
sometimes in the still, small sound
we hear your voice,
proclaiming, whispering,
softly urging your will.

Attune our ears to hear
and our hearts to listen.
Give us discernment
and a new understanding.
Then incline our wish and will,
to joyfully and obediently
do your bidding
when we leave this place.
Amen.

YOUR PLANS, WILL AND CONTROL – NOT MINE

Lord of my life –
I wish for the world
when I go on retreat.
I have such high expectations;
such a list of all that I think
needs to be achieved.

But may your will, Jesus,
and not mine,
fill and gently rule this time.

Help me to let go
of my plans, my control.
May *you* direct this retreat – and not me.
I ask this in your name.
Amen.

No fear

'Do not be afraid.'
So often you said these words
to those who turned to you.
So, Jesus,
I shall not be afraid
as I come,
with a heart full of love
and a mind
wide open to receive.
Amen.

A blessing

May the Silence of God
enfold you.

May the Love of God
surround you.

May the Wisdom of God
teach you.

May the Hand of God
hold you.

May the Blessing of God
rest upon you,
through every moment
of this retreat.
Amen.

CLOSING PRAYERS

YOU STAYED CLOSE BY

Ever constant God,
thank you for this time.
Through the ups and downs,
the lows and highs,
you stayed close by
and enfolded us
in your loving presence.

Bless our return
to the everyday world.
May our gratitude
for these hours/days
be reflected in all
that we are and do.
Amen.

A BLESSING-FILLED TIME

Generous God,
this has been a precious,
blessing-filled time;
time in which to step aside
from daily preoccupations;
time to spend with you,
our Creator and Redeemer,
our saving grace.
Amen.

WALK WITH US AS WE GO FROM THIS PLACE

Jesus,
walk with each one of us
as we go from this place.

Guide our steps;
may they be true.

May we walk
only in your way.

As you have blessed us,
so may we be
a blessing to others.

Make us channels of your
love and peace.

We ask this in your name.
Amen.

A BLESSING ON THOSE WHO MADE THIS TIME POSSIBLE

Jesus,
we ask your blessing
on those who have made this time possible
and attended to all our needs:
for all the work of planning,
for the food and drink so lovingly prepared,
for those who have led the prayer, reflection and worship,
so all we had to do
was concentrate on you,
our Saviour and our friend.
Amen.

YOU BADE ME COME

Heavenly Father,
you called my name.
You bade me come.
How very richly
you have rewarded my obedience.
Thank you.
Amen.

OUR RETREAT-OFFERING

Lord,
we hope we have used
this precious time right
and according to your wish and will.
Forgive the wasted moments.
Gather up the fragments
that are pleasing to you:
these are our retreat-offering.
Amen.

SOUNDS OF SILENCE

Jesus,
the sounds of silence fell on my ears
with the softness of snowflakes,
and every bit as beautiful.
Thank you for opening me
to that wonder-filled experience.

Silence and speech:
both are precious gifts from the Creator,
to be treasured and used
to his greater glory.
Amen.

THANK YOU

Thank you for this time.
Thank you for your care.
Thank you for your guidance.
Thank you for your love.
Amen.

PAUL'S PRAYER

I get down on my knees before the Father,
this magnificent Father
who parcels out all heaven and earth.
I ask him to strengthen you
by his Spirit –
not a brute strength
but a glorious inner strength –
that Christ will live in you
as you open the door and invite him in.
And I ask him that
with both feet planted firmly on love,
you'll be able to take in with all Christians
the extravagant dimensions of Christ's love.
Reach out
and experience the breadth!
Test its length!
Plumb the depths!
Rise to the heights!
Live full lives, full in the fullness of God.
God can do anything, you know –
far more than you could ever imagine
or guess or request
in your wildest dreams!
He does it not by pushing us around
but by working within us,
his Spirit deeply and gently within us.

(Ephesians 3:14f The Message)

USEFUL ADDRESSES

GENERAL

The Compassionate Friends
53 North Street
Bristol BS3 1EN

Helpline: 0117 953 9639
Admin: 0117 966 5202
Fax: 0117 966 5202

Friendship and understanding for bereaved parents whose children have died at any age and from any cause.

Crossroads Care Schemes Ltd
10 Regent Place
Rugby CV21 2PN

Tel: 01788 573653

Cruse Bereavement Care (Branches Nationwide)
National Office:
Cruse House
126 Sheen Road
Richmond
Surrey TW9 1UR

Tel: 020 8940 4818

Counselling and advice for all bereaved people.

Relate (Marriage Guidance)
Herbert Gray College
Little Church Street
Rugby CV21 3AP

Tel: 01788 573241
Fax: 01788 535007

Salvation Army Counselling Service
18 Thanet Street
London WC1H 9QL

Tel: 020 8536 5480

Samaritans
Tel: 0345 909090

A listening ear at any time, 365 days a year, for the price of a local call.

CHILDREN AND FAMILIES

Childline
2nd Floor,
Royal Mail Building,
Studd Street,
London N1 0QW

or:

Freepost 1111
London N1 0BR

Freephone: 0800 1111

Gingerbread
16-17 Clerkenwell Close,
London EC1R 0AA

Helpline: 020 7488 9300

Single parent support group. Local branches nationwide.

(National) Association of Family Mediation and Conciliation Services
50 Westminster Bridge Road,
London SE1 7QY

National Council for One Parent Families
255 Kentish Town Road
London NW5 2LX

Tel: 0800 0185 026

NSPCC Child Protection Helpline: 0800 800 500

National free 24-hour telephone service receiving referrals and offering counselling and advice on child protection matters. The NSPCC offers a range of services to children and their families. Its network of over 100 protection teams and projects undertake activities including investigations, assessment and therapeutic work, family care and training. A consultation service is provided to other child care professionals and for specialist work.

CHILDREN WITH SPECIAL NEEDS

Contact a Family
16 Stratton Ground
London SW1P 2HP

Tel: 020 7383 3555

Self-help for families with disabled or ill children.

National Youth Agency
17-23 Albion Street
Leicester LE1 6GD

Tel: 01533 471200

DISABILITY AND ILLNESS

Break
20 Hooks Hill Road
Sheringham NR26 8NL

Tel: 01263 823170
Fax: 01263 825560

Holidays and respite care for children and adults.

DIAL (National Association of Disablement Advice and Information Lines)
Park Lodge
St Catherine's Hospital
Tickhill Road
Doncaster DN4 8QN

Tel: 01302 310123

Mental Health Media Council
380-384 Harrow Road
London W9 2HU

Information and advice.

THE ELDERLY

Age Concern, England
Astral House
1268 London Road
London SW16 4ER

Tel: 020 8765 7200

Help the Aged
St James' Walk
London EC1R 0BE

Helpline: 0800 289404 (10am-4pm, Monday-Friday)

ADDICTION AND DEPENDENCY

ACCEPT (Addiction Community Centres for Education, Prevention and Treatment)
200 Seagrave Road
London SW16 1RQ

Tel: 020 7381 3155

Alcohol Concern
275 Grays Inn Road
London WC1X 8QF

DAIS (Drugs Advice and Information Service)
38 West Street
Brighton BN1 2RE

Tel: 01273 21000

National Alcohol Helpline
Weddel House
7th Floor
13-14 West Smithfield
London EC1A 9DL

Release
388 Old Street
London EC1V 9LT

24-hour emergency helpline: 020 7603 8654

Information and advice for users, their friends and families.

APPENDIX

**NAME OF CHURCH
OR RETREAT ORGANISERS**

INVITE YOU TO JOIN US ON A

RETREAT

THEME ....

DATE(S) ....

FROM .... TO ....

VENUE ....

COST ....

REDUCED PRICE FOR YOUNG PEOPLE/STUDENTS/RETIRED/UNEMPLOYED ....

**A wonderful opportunity to step aside from
the pressures and preoccupations of everyday life
in order to spend some time just with God.**

FOR FURTHER DETAILS, PLEASE CONTACT

**NAME AND
CONTACT DETAILS**

PRO-FORMA BOOKING FORM

> ## NAME OF CHURCH
> ## OR RETREAT ORGANISERS

RETREAT

DATE ....

FROM .... TO ....

VENUE ....

NAME (PLEASE PRINT) ....

ADDRESS ....

TEL. .... EMAIL ....

WOULD LIKE TO COME ON THE RETREAT.

I ENCLOSE THE REQUIRED DEPOSIT OF ....

SPECIAL NEEDS

DIETRY ....

ACCESS ....

OTHER ....

SIGNED ....

FOR RETREATANTS AGED 16 OR UNDER:

I AGREE TO .... ATTENDING THE ABOVE RETREAT.

SIGNED .... (PARENT OR GUARDIAN)

PLEASE RETURN COMPLETED FORM AND DEPOSIT TO ....

NO LATER THAN .... THANK YOU.

BE STILL,

AND KNOW

THAT

I AM GOD

(PSALM 46:10)